MW01295681

INFORMATION TECHNOLOGY ESSENTIALS

Eric Frick

Published by Eric Frick 2017

Last Update May 2019

Copyright

Table of Contents

Foreword

Hello and welcome to the book! This book is intended to be an introduction to information technology concepts and is based on a video class that I have created on the same topic. The structure of this book is based on a class that I have taught on many occasions that was an introduction to IT for business students at the college level.

Supporting Material

By purchasing this book you will also have free access to the video version of this class. Use the code **itebook** to get free access. You access this class at the following address:

https://destinlearning.com/courses/ite

This is a complete online class that is a companion to this book with videos, downloadable pdf files and online quizzes. If you have suggestions for additions to this book/class I would love to hear from you. You can contact me at:
sales@destinlearning.com

1.0 Introduction

Hello everyone and welcome to Information Technology Essentials. I have put this book together as a part of a series of books for entry-level computer science students. Becoming a software developer requires much more than just knowing how to write programs. This is the first book in the series and starts with the basics of information technology. This book contains the material that a typical entry-level class that a first-year computer science student would take.

This book will start with a history of computing and will also include information about the IT industry in general. Following this, I have included a lesson to give you a basic understanding of how a computer functions from the hardware standpoint. After looking at computer hardware, we will look at the basic operations of a computer network and how the internet is structured.

After looking for basic hardware operations, we will then look at computer software. We will look at the software development lifecycle that software development teams use to build software. We will also see how the computer operating system functions, which is the primary software that runs your computer.

The next section will cover cloud computing and why it is essential in the IT industry today. We will discuss primary definitions of cloud computing and also look at some of the top cloud computing companies in the market today.

I have also included a section on basic computer security. Computer security has become increasingly important in the computer science field and touches almost everyone daily. We will look at the primary threats out in the market today and the general strategies for securing computers.

In the final section, we touch on the future of computing. We will look at some emerging technologies and some of the hot areas of information technology today. By the end of this class, you should have a firm grasp of the basic concepts of information technology that will give you a solid introduction and provide a great background before you start studying more detailed computer science subjects.

For this class, you will only need a computer with a web browser. We will not need to install any additional software to work the lab exercises. The quizzes and labs are available online at my website.

http://destinlearning.com/infotech

2.0 Background

The information technology business today has become one of the most important industries in our worldwide economy. Computers and automation touch almost every aspect of our modern lives. The adoption of the cell phone has been the fastest adoption of technology the world has ever seen. All major corporations in the world today run large-scale IT operations to run their businesses. And most of us utilize computers and software in our personal lives.

In this chapter, I will drill down into more detail about information technology in general. I will start with a discussion of why you would want to study information technology and the benefits behind it. In the next discussion, I will present a brief history of computing and describe some of the significant milestones achieved along the way. This material will build a foundation I will build on for the remainder of the topics in this book.

2.1 Why Study Information Technology?

In this section, I will discuss why you would want to study information technology. I will talk about some of the market factors that make information technology such an important subject and why you would want to study the subject. So, let's get started.

Why study information technology? You are part of the most connected society of all time. The amount of interaction we have with computer systems in our daily lives has grown dramatically over the last few years. Particularly with younger generations, computers are used by most people throughout their daily routine. Information technology touches almost every aspect of your life.

Most workers today interact with computers as part of their job. Personnel that does not work in an IT position still generally depend on information systems to perform their job functions. Even if you are not intending to become part of the IT industry, having a basic knowledge of information systems and information technology will help you to become an informed user. Informed users make better choices and become more valuable to the company.

If you intend to become part of the IT industry, there are many career opportunities and a wide variety of jobs. In many areas of the world, there is a shortage of qualified personnel to fill IT positions. Understanding information technology is a critical first step in becoming a skilled IT worker.

Even if you do not work in an IT company or organization, you will have IT projects and operations, and it is likely that you will at some point become involved with them. Again, understanding information systems will help you become a more effective team member in these projects.

Computing has changed dramatically over the last few years and devices that were only science-fiction ten or twenty years ago are now commonplace. One term that defines the modern world is ubiquitous computing, that is computing that is made to appear anywhere at any time. Most people in developed countries in the world now have multiple computing devices such as cell phones, tablets, wearable devices, desktop computers and other types of systems. Also, there are now many smart devices on the market, and the list of these is growing every day.

Many computer systems are now at work 24 hours a day, seven days a week, 365 days a year. This has created a large demand for data center personnel to maintain these systems.

Many devices are also coming online through a technology called the Internet of things or IoT. These devices allow computer systems to control a large variety of devices from kitchen appliances, lights, manufacturing equipment, etc. Because of this, there is an increased demand for software for command control systems to run these devices.

Younger generations have grown up with this technology and have developed the lifestyle around using mobile devices on the internet. This lifestyle is causing a significant demand for information technology development and services.

The market for information technology systems is enormous. As of 2016, there were over 2 billion smartphones in use worldwide. Also, as of 2000 80% of US households had a personal computer. These statistics would have been unimaginable 30 years ago.

Besides, the price of computer hardware has dropped dramatically, so now devices are becoming more and more affordable as the cost of computer hardware continues to decline.

Due to this increased market demand, IT companies have grown considerably. Google, Apple, and Microsoft are three of the top valued companies in the world. Information Technology services and software development make up much of our economy. With all this growth in demand, there are great opportunities for information-technology workers. In many areas of the world there is a shortage of personnel and filling jobs is difficult. To fill these shortages private training programs such as IT developer boot camps are in growing to fill to void. In addition, pay for information technology workers remains relatively high. Computer programmers made an average salary of $84,360 in 2015. I should note this is from an article I found on US news, and it is only for US-based workers.

Salaries depend highly on the part of the world you live in and the part of the country you live in as well. So even if wages are lower in other parts of the world, the demand for computer programmers in information technology workers remains strong.

And so even if you were not intending to become an information technology worker, being an informed user will help you today. All companies and organizations have basic information technology systems and operations and understanding information basic technology will help you in your daily job. Also, the world is rapidly changing the manner in which news outlets distribute information has changed dramatically due to new technology developments.

Remote workplaces are now becoming more commonplace. Many workers now telecommute from their homes to work. New computer devices are continually introduced at a rapid pace as technology continues to evolve. Companies and organizations must commit to ongoing training to help their workers stay up with new technology.

In summary, the IT business is growing at a rapid pace and presents excellent opportunities for IT personnel worldwide. Technology is continually changing, and companies introduce new products and services almost on a daily basis. Being an informed user is a must in today's rapidly changing world. Understanding information technology will help you no matter which direction your career is taking you. I hope this chapter has given you some motivation to understand the importance of studying computer science and information technology in today's world.

3.0 Computer Hardware

Advances in computer hardware have fueled the explosive growth in the computing revolution. The advances in computer hardware over the last fifty years has been nothing short of amazing. Computers are consistently faster, smaller and more affordable. These advances have fueled the worldwide explosion in affordable computer products of all kinds and have also created an enormous demand for new software applications to run on these machines.

In this chapter, I will describe some fundamental information about computer hardware. First, I will start with the basic operation of a computer. I will explain the major components of a computer and the functions they provide to the system. I will also describe how these components interact with each other to produce a working system. Next, I will explain the different types of computers that are in use today. Following that, I will discuss Moore's Law and how that law has succeeded in predicting the sustained growth in computing power. In the last section of this chapter, I will present a short explanation of binary numbers which is the basis of how all modern computer operate. Following this explanation, we will conclude this chapter with a brief exercise with binary number conversion.

3.1 How Does a Computer Work?

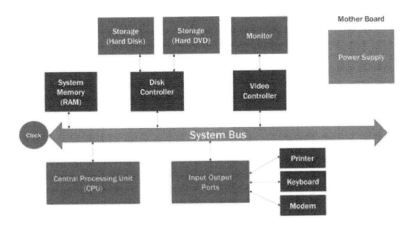

In this section, I will give an overview of the components of a computer and how they function. This lesson will provide a high-level overview of the major components of a computer system and how they interact together. So, let's get started.

Motherboard

The first major component of any computer system is the motherboard. The motherboard is the baseline component that gives the structure to the computer. The motherboard allows components to be secured to it and gives it the electrical power for operation.

Along with the motherboard, the power supply distributes power to each component of the computer system.

System Bus

The system bus is one of the fundamental components that allows all the components of a computer system to communicate with each other. Integral to the system bus is the system clock which coordinates and times the operations for the computer. These two components work together to make sure that the operations are properly sequenced and synchronized.

CPU

The next major component is the central processing unit or CPU. The CPU is the brain of the computer and performs mathematical computations necessary to operate programs on the computer. Much of the speed of a computer is a result of the clock speed and the processing capabilities of the central processing unit.

RAM

For a computer to effectively run programs, these programs are loaded by the operating system into the system memory or RAM. RAM stands for random access memory. The amount of RAM and the size and speed of the system bus also determine the overall processing speed of the computer system. If you have more RAM in a computer, it will allow you to operate more programs simultaneously. Over the last few years, computers have consistently increased in speed and capacity due to advances in computer hardware.

Disk Controller

The operating system loads programs in and out of memory via the disk controller. The disk controller will synchronize operations with storage devices such as a hard disk or DVD drive. Larger desktop computers may have multiple hard disks and or DVD drives.

Video Controller

Programs display output on a monitor via a video controller. Some controllers may support a system with multiple monitors. Also, video controllers may support special function and high-resolution graphics to support special uses such as video gaming and engineering and architectural applications.

Other types of external devices are connected to the computer by input and output ports. In this way, devices such as printers, keyboards and pointing devices such as a mouse are connected to the system using USB cables. It is also possible to connect a modem in this manner. Devices such as cable modems allow computers to have access to the Internet.

This picture is an example of what a typical motherboard looks like for a desktop computer. You can see the motherboard has slots for mounting CPU and memory chips as well as the input and output ports located along the back of the motherboard. The power supply is not pictured in this and is generally included with the case for the computer. Notebook computers have the same components as a desktop computer but are not as modular as desktop computers since they are optimized for the smaller size of a mobile device.

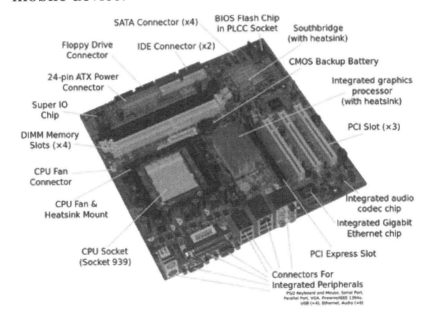

3.2 Hardware Quiz

In this exercise, you will select the best match for these items from the list presented below.

_____	Power Supply
_____	CPU
_____	Motherboard
_____	RAM
_____	Hard Disk
_____	System Bus

A. The central processing unit for a computer
B. Primary storage for all programs and data
C. Local memory used to execute running programs
D. Supplies primary power to all the computer's components
E. Used to communicate between the computer system's components
F. Provides the structure to mount the major system components

3.3 What are the Different Types of Computers?

In this section, I will describe the different computers that are in use today. If I wrote this chapter thirty years ago, this list would have been much shorter. Let's get started.

Today there are a huge number of different computers in use today, but they generally fall into a few categories. Since the cost of computer hardware has come down significantly and the size of the components is much smaller, it is much easier to include computers in devices unable to take advantage of the capability a few years ago. As this trend continues, more types of devices are frequently being introduced to the market by computer companies.

With all of these different devices, let's look and see what the major types are.

- Desktop Computers
- Laptop Computers
- Tablets
- Smart Phones
- Servers
- Mainframe Computers
- Embedded Systems
- Wearable Devices

Now we will take a brief look at each one.

Desktop Computer

The first computer type on the list is the desktop computer. These computers were introduced in the 1980s and have been a mainstay of the market since then. Businesses still use these devices heavily and are used for everyday computing for office automation. Home users still use these them but the market shifted to laptop computers in the mid-2000s. The sales of desktop computers have steadily fallen year after year since then. Major manufacturers of these devices include Dell, HP, and Apple.

Laptop Computer

The next computer on the list is the Laptop Computer. These were designed to be a small, portable personal computer. These devices continue to improve in speed and processing power as the technology improves. Also, these devices continue to become lighter with improved battery life. Major manufacturers of these devices include Acer, Dell, Apple, and Toshiba.

Smart Phone

Several years after introducing the laptop computer, the smartphone dominated the market. These devices are cell phones that provide an advanced mobile operating system. Smartphones offer these capabilities:

- Phone
- Camera (including video)
- GPS
- Touch Screen

The growth in the adoption of these devices has been incredible. There are over two billion devices in use today. Most of these devices utilize the IOS operating system from Apple or the Android operating system from Google. Major manufacturers include Apple, Samsung, LG, and Google.

Tablet computer

The tablet computer was made famous by Apple Computer when they introduced the iPad. Table computers use a touch screen and rarely include a keyboard (although most vendors offer a separate attachable keyboard as an add-on option) Since the extreme popularity of the iPad, tablet computer models have been introduced by other manufacturers such as Samsung, HP, and Acer. Also, most competitors to the iPad run the Google Android operating system.

Server

The next computer on the list is the server. Servers became popular during the rise in popularity of the internet and the World Wide Web. These computers provide functionality for programs or devices called clients.

Servers provide functionality for applications such as:

- Databases
- File servers
- Email servers
- Web servers
- Application servers

Servers are clustered so new servers can be added to increase capacity easily (server farm). Manufacturers include Dell, HP, IBM, and Oracle.

Mainframe

Mainframe computers have been developed since the late 1950s and were some of the earliest computers in use in the industry. These computers run large mission-critical applications, such as banking and ERP systems. These machines are fast and highly reliable. They are also designed to handle applications that require high input and output. Major vendors of mainframes include IBM, Unisys, and Hitachi.

Embedded Systems

Since computer hardware is much cheaper, computers are being integrated into a wide variety of devices to name a few:
- Aircraft
- Weapon systems
- Automobiles
- Gaming systems
- GPS systems
- Robotic systems
- Manufacturing systems
- Vision systems

Computer companies are now introducing more devices through a technology called the Internet of Things or IoT. You will hear more about these devices as this technology matures.

Wearable Devices

The last computer we will talk about is the wearable device. These are designed to be worn by the user under, with, or on top of clothing. There are already many devices already on the market. These include:

- Fitbit
- Apple Watch
- Google Glass
- Body Cams

As this market evolves, there are more devices under development.

In summary, there has been an explosion of new devices introduced over the last decade. The good news for programmers and IT workers is these devices require software to run them and provide opportunities for developers. The list of new devices is growing every day. As hardware prices continue to drop, these devices continue to become better, cheaper and faster.

3.4 Moore's Law

Ever since the introduction of computers, the hardware has consistently gotten faster, smaller and cheaper. The processing power available on most cell phones today would have been unthinkable just ten years ago. Newer, faster, and more capable devices are rolled out at an unbelievable pace. Introducing these devices has changed how we lead our daily lives.

In 1968, Gordon Moore, pictured above, co-founded Intel and became part of the movement that created the first ever microprocessor. Microprocessors are the heart of today's computing devices, and Intel is one of the leading microprocessor manufacturers in the world.

While working at Intel, Moore noticed a pattern in the growth of computing. He found that the number of transistors per square inch had doubled every year since the invention of integrated circuits. So, he developed Moore's law that predicts that computing power would double every year. In 1975, he revised the estimate to every two years.

The model that Moore developed has been remarkably consistent over the last fifty years. Computers continue to become faster and more capable. Many people debate if Moore's law will continue to be valid. Some people believe this trend will not continue and we are pushing the laws of physics. The critical point of this discussion is there has been a well-established model that has consistently predicted the growth of computing power and has been accurate for the last half-century.

Although the rate of growth might slow somewhat, there is no evidence this trend of growth of computing power will not continue for the foreseeable future.

3.5 Binary Numbers

Modern computers are digital computers, that is they have an architecture that processes binary numbers for all of their calculations. As human beings, we are more used to dealing with a decimal (base 10) numbering system. We have ten fingers, so this is a natural way of counting and processing math for us. Computers on the other have are based on electronic circuitry and because of this they implement a binary system. Considering computers are based on electricity and electricity can either be one or off, a way of counting based on that on (1) or off (0) was devised. It is much easier to implement circuits to process binary information than a base 10 type of architecture.

To fully understand the basic operations of a digital computer, you must understand the binary numbering system and how to convert binary numbers to decimal and also convert decimal numbers to binary. The Central Processing Unit or CPU of a computer processes all of its operations as binary instructions. Computer programmers write the lowest level computer programs in assembly language which are then translated into machine language by an assembler. To be proficient in this type of programming, you must understand binary numbers.

In this book, it is not my goal for you to learn assembly language programming, but I do want you to have a basic understanding of how modern computers operate and the basic principles. Teaching basic binary numbers and math operations is a topic that all computer science students should understand.

The Binary Numbering System

Binary numbers are also referred to as bits. These bits are the lowest level of storage on a digital computer. A bit is either a 1 or a 0 (also referred to as on and off). Listed in the table below are the first ten decimal numbers and their binary equivalents.

Decimal	Binary (Nibble)
1	0001
2	0010
3	0011
4	0100
5	0101
6	0110
7	0111

8	1000
9	1001
10	1010

Do you notice the pattern when counting from 1 to 10 in binary? Each digit represents a power of 2 in each digits position starting from 0 for the left-most digit to the right. Also, there are 8 bits in a byte which is the fundamental storage unit of a computer's memory. A nibble is half of that or 4 bits.

The following binary number:

011 represents

$= 0^{*3} + 1^{*2} + 1^{*}2^0$

$= 0 + 2 + 1$

$= 3$

Convert from Binary to Decimal

To convert a binary number to decimal, we can do the conversion by multiplying the value of each digit d_n by d_n, for n from 0 (the least significant digit) to n-1 (the most significant digit) for an n digit number, and by summing all the products obtained in this way. The following is an example:

Convert $(1101)_2$ to decimal.

Solution:

$$(1101)_2 = (1 * 2^3) + (1 * 2^2) + (0 * 2^1) + (1 * 2^0)$$

$$= (1 * 8) + (1 * 4) + (0 * 1) + (1 * 1)$$

$$= 8 + 4 + 0 + 1$$

$$= 13$$

Convert From Decimal to Binary

To convert a decimal number to binary, you go through a division process. Start with the original number and divide it by 2 and the recorded the remainder and the record the result of that division on the next line. Keep doing this division until you reach zero. The following is an example of converting $(221)_{10}$ to binary.

Divisor	Quotient	Reminder
2	221	1
2	110	0
2	55	1
2	27	1
2	13	1
2	6	0
2	3	1
2	1	1
2	0	

Now, if we write the remainders in order from the last one obtained, to the first one obtained, we have: $(221)_{10} = (11011101)_2$.

You have now seen the process of how binary number work and how to do some basic conversions. Most digital computers today store and process their information in 32 bits or 64 bits. The larger the number of bits a computer utilizes they can do larger computations in a single cycle and get more work done. The sizes of the calculation have grown steadily over the years. Early personal computers processed only 8 bits at a time.

Online Conversion Programs

There are many online converters that you can utilize to convert large binary numbers to decimal. These sites can also do other conversions as well. Pictured below is a screenshot of one of these programs. You can click on the following URL to try this program out on your own.

https://www.binaryhexconverter.com/binary-to-decimal-converter

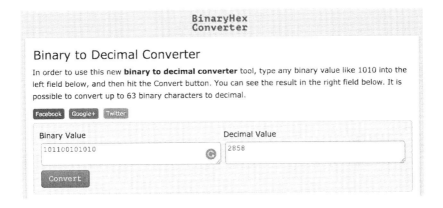

3.6 Binary Numbers Quiz

1) Convert the decimal number 153 to binary. (do not use the conversion web page)

2) What is the following binary number 0011 0011 to decimal. (do not use the conversion web page)

3) Convert the following 32-bit binary number using the conversion web page.
https://www.binaryhexconverter.com/binary-to-decimal-converter
0101 1100 1010 0001 0000 1010 1100 0101

4) Convert the following decimal number to binary using the conversion web page.
https://www.binaryhexconverter.com/decimal-to-binary-converter
45,649

5) Most modern computer process information with 32 or 64 bits
   a) True
   b) False

4.0 Computer Networking

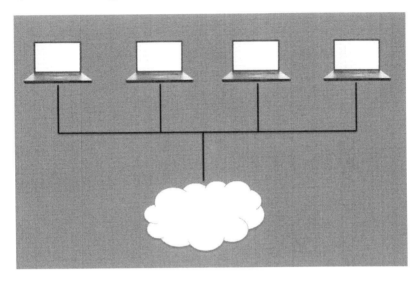

Computer networks allow systems to extend their reach and interact with other computers and users on their local area network. If their network is connected to the internet, then users will have access to software and services worldwide. Computer networking is a very important part of information technology and the demand for network hardware and services has exploded since introducing the internet. In recent years we have not only seen a huge growth in wired networks, but we have also seen an explosion in the growth of wireless networks with the worldwide adoption of the cell phone.

Network engineers are highly paid employees and are in great demand. In addition, software engineers and designers must have basic knowledge of network functions so when they design and program software systems, they function properly in a network environment.

In this chapter, I will describe the basics of computer networking. First, I will describe a brief history of computer networking and some of the basic terminology. Next, I will describe the basic operation of a local area network or LAN. This is the basic building block of computer networks and is now very commonplace. Finally, I will describe the basic components that comprise the internet and how they work together to form today's Internet.

4.1 The History of Computer Networking

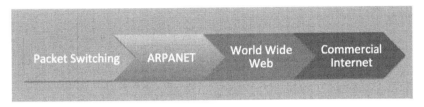

The average person uses a computer network in almost every aspect of modern everyday life in developed countries. Many people now take the use of these services for granted. Most of us today have instant access to services that can connect us to a worldwide variety of online goods and services instantly from a wide range of devices.

The infrastructure for these networks is a product of advancements that have taken place over the last thirty to forty years of computing and innovation. These innovations have come from research and development that has taken place in universities, the military, and commercial environments. The resulting technologies combined have resulted in one of the most amazing events in human history: the birth and growth of the internet. From the simple beginnings of research and development projects in the 1960s, the internet today connects a large percentage of the world's population to online goods and services.

In these following sections, I will outline some of the key projects and technologies that have provided some of the foundational elements of today's modern networks and the Internet. Each element provides some of the critical components that allow the widespread use of the commercial internet today.

Packet Switching

In the early 1960s, several groups researched packet switching to allow computers to communicate with each other. Until that time, circuit switching had been a method for computer communications. Through the work of several research groups at MIT, the Rand Institute, and the National Physical Laboratory in England, they developed some of the basic concepts that the internet uses today.

ARPANET

In the late 1970s, work that was sponsored by the Defense Advanced Research Project Agency or DARPA developed a network of computers called ARPANET. This effort developed a method for different computers to communicate with each other. This research included computers from both military installations and research universities. The project grew from an initial set of a handful of machines to hundreds in the early 1980s. The structure and growth of the ARPANET provided the basic model for the internet today.

TCP/IP

The underlying protocol the internet uses today for network traffic is called TCP/IP. It stands for Transmission Control Protocol/Internet Protocol. The TCP/IP protocol was developed by two scientists, Vint Cerf, and Bob Kahn while working for the Defense Advanced Research Project Agency. They migrated the ARPA network to this protocol and eventually migrated the entire system to this protocol in 1983. TCP/IP eventually became the standard for all military networks. Besides this research work, they published their work in RFC standards that allowed TCP/IP to move into the public domain. This work provided the basis for the networking standards still in use today.

World Wide Web (WWW)

Tim Berners-Lee who worked at CERN, the European Organization for Nuclear Research invented the worldwide web or WWW in the 1989-1990 time frame. CERN and Tim Berners-Lee developed the first web server and was driven by the need for researchers around the world to share information. After the first web server was developed, CERN published instructions on how other institutions could set up their own web servers. These instructions resulted in several hundred other institutions hosting their own web servers. In 1993 CERN opened the code for the web servers and the browser to the public domain and made the software freely available. Once the software was in the public domain, it provided the basis for the explosive growth of the World Wide Web and the internet that was to follow.

4.2 How Does a Local Area Network Function?

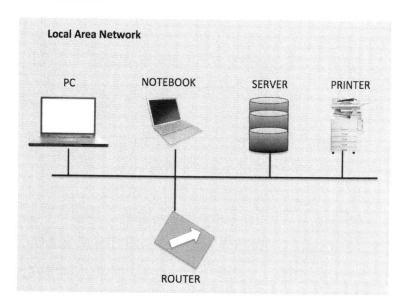

Local Area Network

PC NOTEBOOK SERVER PRINTER

ROUTER

A local area network or LAN is in a limited area. A LAN is typically in a single location such as a single office building, a school, or even a home office. Computers and devices are connected via Ethernet and connect with some network cables and router. Typically, the cabling used in most home and offices networks is called Category 5 or Cat 5.

These cables are usually connected with connectors referred to as RJ45 connectors. This allows the cables to be simply plugged into devices. The following figure is a picture of a Cat 5 cable with an RJ45 connector.

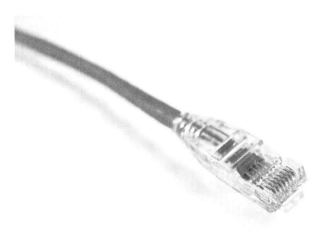

Services

Local area networks allow users to access shared services within their group. A workgroup or a domain defines the group depending on the setup and operating system the network is using. The LAN allows users to share physical devices such are printers, scanners and any other devices connected to the network. This setup enables companies and home users to lower cost by allowing users to share expensive devices such as high-speed color printers.

Besides shared devices, LANs also allows users to share files and information. Shared network drives provide a common area for storing files. These file shares can be configured to secure the access to specific files by the way user groups and file permissions. System administrators grant these right by way of group permissions. For example, accounting users can only write files to an area on a file share that only members of the Accounting Department can access.

A LAN might also provide access to email services. One server on the network might be an email server to allow users within the group to send email messages to each other. This setup was very popular several years ago. However, more companies are moving their email system to cloud services such as Google G Suite and Office 365.

Routers

Routers are the devices on the network that allow these devices to talk to each other and provide the underlying communication services. Routers provide the network services that relay the network traffic from one device to another. These devices are usually highly configurable and allow the IT staff to configure them to route the traffic efficiently between devices and also to help secure the network to help keep unwanted traffic off of the network.

Routers have become more powerful over the last few years, and the cost of these devices has also dropped. Some devices also integrate into wireless access as well and allow users on the LAN to communicate through a wireless connection. Many home networking packages come pre-configured in this way, so the networking service only needs to provide a single device to their home networking customers. The following figure shows a photo of a typical router that can that is used for home networking applications.

4.3 How Does the Internet Work?

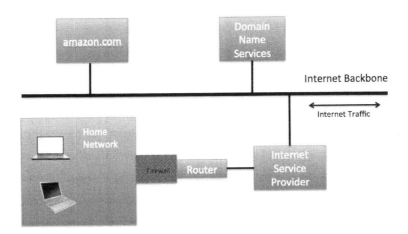

In this chapter, I will explain how the internet functions in some simple terms. The internet is an example of a wide area network or WAN. Although the scale and size of this WAN are unprecedented, it still primarily functions as a WAN.

A WAN operates over a wide geographic area. Also, a WAN can comprise many Local Area Networks, or LANs described in the previous section. Internet users connect their home systems to the internet via an Internet Service

Provider or ISP. In the early days of the Internet, users directly connected a single computer to the internet. Now it is much more common to connect a home network to the internet. In this way, a device with connectivity to your home network can then have access to the internet.

Connectivity

Your Internet Service Provider (ISP) provides a device such as a cable modem or DSL modem to connect to the Internet. The type of device will depend on the technology that your ISP is using to connect to their home customers. Also, these devices will provide firewall services to help secure the connection to your local area network. These firewalls can block access to certain types of network traffic when properly configured.

When using your home network, if you generate any network traffic that is supposed to go to the Internet, the router will then forward this information to your ISP. Once the data gets to your ISP, it will then be forwarded to the Internet Backbone to get to the desired destination. The Internet backbone is a high-speed network that routes network traffic to the correct destination.

Protocols

One reason the internet has been so successful is that the network traffic is based on standard network protocols that have been agreed to by various standards bodies. Two of the major protocols in use today are:

- TCP/IP and
- HTTP

TCP/IP is the network protocol that allows network traffic to be broken into packets and routed over a network. These packets have the source, destination and the information they are moving contained in various segments of the packets. Your computer constructs these packets and then sent across the internet to the destination computer where the packets are decoded and interpreted. This transformation is transparent to the users of these systems but allows for the efficient transmission of a wide variety of network traffic. The basis for TCP/IP was developed in the early days of network research and is now in widespread use on the internet. TCP stands for Transmission Control Protocol. IP stands for Internet Protocol.

HTTP is the data that is sent by servers on the Internet to your web browser. HTTP stands for Hyper Text Transmission Protocol. HTTP defines how web servers structure and transmit information out to your home computer and how your browser can then render that information. These standards have been in place since the early days of the world-wide-web, and now constitute a major portion of the traffic on the Internet today.

Domain Name Service

The primary communication method of TCP/IP uses an IP address for connecting one computer to another. These IP addresses are in the form of a four-part number. An example of an IP address is 10.12.105.10. These addresses are not easy for humans to remember. It is much easier for us to remember names such as amazon.com. Domain name service is the service on the Internet that maps these names to addresses. In this way, you never have to know the IP address of the server or service, only the domain name. There are domain name servers on the internet that provide this translation service and keep the mapping of these names, and IP addresses up to date so users can reliably reach their destination.

Companies must register and purchase their domain names from Domain Registrars. There are many companies today on the Internet you can use to buy domain names. The big problem now is that companies and organizations have already purchased some of the popular names, so it is becoming harder to get the name you might want to purchase. Besides the name you purchase, your organization will also fall into a larger part of the domain naming service. Several popular high-level domains in use are:

- .com for commercial companies
- .gov for government organizations
- .edu for universities and educational institutions and
- .org for nonprofit organizations

There are many other extensions in use and more on the way, but the list presented above are some of the main ones that are in use today.

I have summarized some of the high-level technology that allows the internet to function. There is more to the mechanics of how a network of millions of computers uses to operate, but the concepts provided here should give you a basis for a high-level understanding of basic networking and a basis for further study.

5.0 Software

Software allows computer systems provide value to their users. As hardware platforms have grown in speed and complexity, software, in general, has also increased in capability. Data-driven websites, mobile apps, and embedded systems now offer users of these systems capabilities we would not have thought possible just a few short years ago.

In this first section, I will describe the general process used to develop software, which is known as the software development lifecycle. Using this process, teams of software engineers run through general steps to produce functioning software. Next, I will discuss E-commerce and the different systems that are in use today. Last, I will discuss enterprise applications. These software systems are used by most major corporations and government agencies to run large parts of their operations today.

5.1 The Software Development Lifecycle

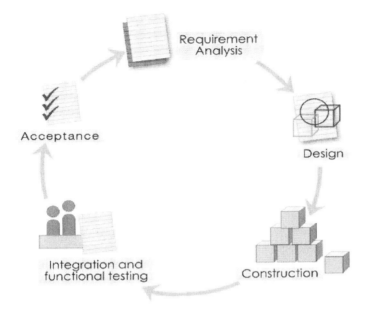

In this section, I will describe the software development lifecycle. I will explain to you the general steps taken to develop software and the definitions of each phase of the software development lifecycle. So, let's get started.

What is the software development lifecycle? The software development lifecycle or SDLC are the general steps taken by software development teams to produce working software. Each step defines a phase of the software development project. During each phase, team members will have different responsibilities that will help drive the software towards final production. Some steps may overlap, but they generally define where the project is regarding developing the final product. If there is difficulty in some steps, then the project may fall back to a previous step to fix the problem. For example, if the team finds severe problems during the test phase, the project may need to go all the way back to the design phase to fix the problem.

Although there are many variations of this process and companies may have their own proprietary model, the following represents the general steps of the SDLC. These are the feasibility study, requirements analysis, design, coding, system testing, deploying, and operations. Now, let's go through each step in more detail and see how they all fit together.

Feasibility Study

The first step in the process is a feasibility study. Some project may skip this process for small projects, but can be a critical step for large ones. In this phase, the project is looked at holistically to determine the general time frame, the approximate budget and the number of staff required. In this phase, the project staff will determine if the project can conforms with the existing company budget and resources. Also, staff may also determine if there is software already on the market that can be purchased by the company, or the IT staff could modify an existing software application instead of developing a custom product. This decision is known as the buy versus build scenario. The outcome of this phase is an approval or rejection from company management whether or not the project will be approved or not. If the project is approved, it will then have an approved budget and timetable.

Requirements Analysis

Once the project is approved, it will then move into the requirements analysis phase. In this phase, the business analyst will build a complete requirements specification to determine the exact functionality of the software. These specifications will include detailed business rules that define the low-level functionality required. It will also include security requirements that the system must support such as the user roles.

You can also include such things as use cases that will define basics usage scenarios for the software. Specifications can also include sample screen designs that will help developers during the coding phase.

Also, this is a good time to define reporting requirements for the system. Requirement gathering teams often overlook the reporting requirements during this process, but this is a great time to include this analysis since they define the specific data you must store in the system. It is much more expensive and complicated to add additional data to the system after it is deployed rather than dealing with it in the requirements phase.

Design

Once the team has completed the requirements specification, the project will move into the design phase. In this phase, designers will map specific requirements into designs. These designs will include both logical models and physical models. The logical model will determine the groupings of software components necessary to meet the basic requirements. Physical designs will consist of hardware elements required to host the software to meet basic usage requirements, such as the number of concurrent users that will be using the system, the availability of the system and the usage scenarios the system must deliver. The physical designs will include server topology, network components, any mobile devices required, and perhaps desktop computers. The design phase tries to provide developers with the information they will need to develop code to meet the basic requirements of the system.

Coding

The next phase is perhaps the most well-known phase of the software development lifecycle, the coding phase. In this phase, programmers will write code to map out all the functionality of the system. Programmers will look to reuse code they have developed on previous projects to save time in their development efforts. Besides developing code, programmers will also develop unit tests at this point to ensure the code meets the basic functional requirements. Also, many projects will begin demonstrations to customers at this point to make sure there are no surprises in the end product. The earlier the problems can be found and identified in the SDLC process the cheaper and easier they are to fix. Once code goes into production, fixing bugs and missed requirements can be very expensive.

System Test

The last major phase of the SDLC before production is the test phase. If projects are running behind schedule and over budget, it is often tempting to cut short on the test phase. Doing this can be a risky proposition and mostly results in programmers delivering a low-quality system. Developing test cases is a critical step in this process. Quality testing will require a high level of participation from the business customers to ensure the system performs well once it goes into production. This process is complicated to do since most organizations have difficulty in sparring additional staff for testing.

After the functionals testing is complete, the testing staff should perform load testing at this point. This testing will determine how well the system will perform during peak demand. Failure to test this can be catastrophic. There have been several high-profile failures in large system development projects that had encountered problems when the system was rolled out under full load conditions. Perhaps the most famous is the US government's launch of the healthcare software that resulted in many frustrated users trying to use a system that performed poorly under high load conditions. Fixing this after the fact was a lengthy, embarrassing and expensive process. This failure is only one of many high-profile software projects that have encountered this problem.

Deploy

Once the testing has successfully completed, the software will be ready to deploy into the production environment. It departments generally scheduled these deployments for off hours or weekends to minimize disruptions of the existing system. Also, large systems may be rolled out in phases of one portion of the system at a time. User training may also take place at this time. Large systems will also require a communication plan to alert users when the new system will go into production and how they must adequately prepare.

Operations

After the system deployment, the system will then go into the operations mode. In this phase the help desk is formed to support users, fix problems, and alert server personnel and programmers about significant issues that users have encountered. Server maintenance and patching will also be scheduled. The maintenance staff schedules routine maintenance operations such as backups, operating system patches, and security patches into the rotation at this point. Although the software is operational most projects will continue to develop new features as the users require them.

This need for future development causes the process to repeat itself. This unplanned development is the cyclical part of the software development process. The problematic issue for company management is that since this process is continuous, it will continue to be an expense to the company. At this point, the company must determine an operating budget for the system. Often the cost for this is underestimated and can become a real nightmare for an organization that has not anticipated this.

Summary

In summary, the SDLC has several distinct steps or phases. Software development projects move from one face to the next after fully completing each one. The IT team may need to repeat some steps if problems occur in a particular phase. Many companies develop their own proprietary models they use during the software development process. Even though they may develop their own process, it is still generally based on the phases described in this chapter.

Understanding the basic steps of the software development life cycle is necessary for any programmer to know since it defines the activities that the project team will perform along the course of a software development project. Software development projects are far more complicated than just writing code. I hope this section has given you a solid understanding of the SDLC.

5.2 SDLC Quiz

1) The buy vs. build decision is made in the Feasibility stage of the SDLC?

    A) True

    B) False

2) In which SDLC phase are both Logical Designs and Physical Designs developed?

    A) Test Phase

    B) Coding Phase

    C) Design Phase

    D) Analysis Phase

3) Is it a good practice to shorten or skip the Test Phase?

    A) True

    B) False

4) Many software development teams give customer demos during the Coding Phase.

    A) True

    B) False

5) It is much cheaper to make bug fixes after the software is in production.

    A) True

    B) False

6) It is impossible in a software development project to repeat a step of the SDLC process.

    A) True

    B) False

5.3 e-Commerce Systems

In this section, I will describe e-commerce. I will explain the basic definition of e-commerce and why it essential in our economy today. I will also describe the significant different e-commerce system operating today.

E-commerce is the business of buying and selling goods online. Since the widespread use of the internet, online purchases have steadily increased. The basis of E-commerce is transactions. There are also many types of transactions that can be performed by many devices. Because of this, e-commerce involves many technologies. These include mobile devices, supply chain management systems, point-of-sale systems, electronic data interchange, and EDI and online transaction processing systems, also known as OLTP. Because of the size and complexity of these systems, they represent excellent opportunities for IT professionals to work on these systems.

E-commerce represents a significant and growing part of the worldwide academy. E-commerce is becoming an increasingly large portion of retail sales. As of the second quarter of 2016, e-commerce accounted for 8.1% of the total retail sales in the United States. In this quarter, sales accounted for over $97 billion in transactions. This statistic shows you the size, growth, and importance of e-commerce in our society today. I should also note these figures are only US-based figures; it does not include the worldwide growth of e-commerce. As you can see, e-commerce is steadily growing and becoming a more critical part of the global economy. It is also a significant part of computer science and software development.

Now that we have looked at the basic definition of e-commerce let's look at the different e-commerce types used today. Included is the general definition of the transactions that major systems utilize today. The first type is business to consumer or B2C e-commerce. These systems allow businesses to make sales to consumers online. The next category is business to business or B2B commerce. These systems enable businesses to automate their sales and purchases to other companies online. Following this is a consumer to business tor C2B types of transactions. These represent a smaller portion of the e-commerce sites but represent a growing number of systems.

The next e-commerce system is the consumer-to-consumer or C2C type of system. These systems allow consumers to sell products and services to other consumers directly. The last type e-commerce system is government to the citizen or G2C types of systems. These systems allow government agencies to automate the delivery of services to citizens online. Now we will look at all of these systems in more detail.

Business to Consumer

B2C systems allow businesses to sell directly to consumers online. Companies like Amazon.com are the most well-known examples of this. Many companies operate both retail locations and web operations simultaneously. For example, companies such as BestBuy have retail locations as well as an online business. This situation can lead to a problem called channel conflict. Using BestBuy as an example, you may go into a retail location and find that a product has a different price in the store then it does online. This difference can present a huge problem for large companies to explain to their customers. It often leaves consumers with a bad experience with the company. Also, many traditional companies have had difficulties in moving to online sales. Traditional brick and mortar companies rarely have the expertise to support the 24/7 nature of online e-commerce systems. These companies, however, must compete with other online retailers as more transactions move online.

Business to Business

The next e-commerce system is B2B or business-to-business e-commerce. These systems allow businesses to automate their buying of goods and services from their business partners. They are designed for high volume purchases and are used to increase supply chain efficiencies. These systems help companies lower cost increase competitiveness. Large companies will often require their business partners to utilize e-commerce systems for them to be a qualified business partner. This requirement can sometimes be a significant problem for small businesses that want to work with larger companies. These systems are becoming more commonplace for even small companies to utilize.

Consumer to Consumer

The next e-commerce I will discuss is the consumer-to-consumer or C2C type of transaction. These systems provide a marketplace so consumers can sell goods and services to other consumers directly. Websites such as eBay are a classic example. These systems provide services such as listing products, shipping, billing, and returns. They allow consumers to offer online products and services with little or no infrastructure. Many of these types of systems will charge a fee to support offering their online services. These systems represent a growing portion of the economy. Craig's List and eBay are classic examples of C2C e-commerce sites.

Government to Citizen

The last e-commerce system is the government to citizen or G2C type of system. These systems allow government agencies to provide essential services electronically rather than traditional form-based or paper-based systems. One of the primary goals is to enable government agencies to lower the cost of the delivery of services. Older paper-based systems required much manual labor which is very expensive in today's market. As government agencies become more challenged with shrinking budgets, they are looking to automation to help lower cost. A typical service in the space might be something like the IRS allowing taxpayers to file their taxes online. Besides filing, the system is also designed to handle online payment. More services are on the way from government agencies as cost becomes a more critical driver in today's economy.

Summary

In summary, e-commerce is an important and growing part of our economy. More companies are pushing to have a large web presence, and online transactions are steadily increasing. This growth is good news for IT professionals since the demand for personnel to develop, operate and maintain these systems is growing.

5.4 e-Commerce Quiz

1) B2B Commerce refers to:
    A) Consumer to Consumer commerce
    B) Business to Business commerce
    C) Business transaction systems

2) B2B commerce is designed for high volume transactions.
    A) True
    B) False

3) Which site is a classic example of C2C commerce?
    A) Delta Airlines
    B) Amazon
    C) eBay

4) Which website is the best example of B2C commerce?
    A) Amazon
    B) Craig's List
    C) eBay

5) G2C refers to?

  A) Government to Citizen commerce
  B) Government automation systems
  C) General transaction to consumers

5.5 Enterprise Applications

In this chapter, I will describe enterprise applications. I will talk about the definition of what an enterprise application is and some examples of the applications that are on the market today.

So why would we want to study enterprise applications? Enterprise applications are commonly used by large companies to run significant portions of their businesses. Because of this, they represent a large segment of the software market. Also, many companies have custom built systems with interfaces to their enterprise systems. Software personnel must routinely build interfaces to move data in and out. Also, these systems require maintenance and operation support from IT departments. Vendors of the systems hire a large workforce to develop, maintain, deploy, and sell these systems. If you pursue a career in information technology, it is likely that you work with one of these systems in some way.

So, what is an enterprise application? These systems are shared resources and designed to be used by the entire organization. This model differs significantly from a system designed to be only used by a single department. These systems solve common business problems for the enterprise. They provide an end to end working solution for that particular business area.

So, what are some advantages of enterprise applications? One of the significant benefits of enterprise applications is they provide business processes already predefined that you can use for your company. These business processes often represent the best-in-class business process that is ready to use. The system provides a standard platform for the company and standardizes business process implementation. This standardization saves companies a lot of effort in trying to design new business processes or fix an existing one. They can simply use the ones that the enterprise application offers.

Although these systems have many advantages, they also have drawbacks. The first disadvantage is, these systems are expensive. Besides, they can be complicated to implement. Many companies also find it difficult to modify all of their business processes to fit into predefined processes offered in these software packages. Another potential problem is these packages can sometimes be difficult to customize and therefore create problems.

Although there are many different enterprise

applications, this list is some of the most common packages in use in the market today. The first and most common enterprises application is the ERP or enterprise resource planning system. The next one listed is the customer relationship or CRM package. Following this is the enterprise content management system or ECM system. Next on the list is the human resource information system or HRIS system. The last system listed is the supply chain management or SCM system. I will now go through each one of these.

ERP Systems

Enterprise resource planning systems or ERP systems represent perhaps the most comprehensive set of enterprise software on the list. The systems are an integrated application that manages most of the back-office functions for a company. The systems are usually modular, and companies can choose which modules they want to implement for their company operations. Some of the more common modules are product planning, production planning, factory automation, inventory, shipping, and finance. Some of the leading vendors in the space are SAP, Oracle, Microsoft, Epicor, and NetSuite.

CRM Systems

The next system we will talk about is the customer relationship management or CRM system. These systems provide a customer-centric view or a 360° view of a customer and how they interact with the company. They assist with customer retention and driving sales growth. Standard features of the systems include marketing automation, sales force automation, and call center automation. Some of the leading vendors in this space are salesforce.com, Oracle, and SAP.

ECM Systems

Enterprise Content Management systems or ECM systems are used to capture, manage, store and deliver content. These functions include both document management and web content management. These systems usually include workflow and document capture and lower cost of traditional paper-based systems. Some of the leading vendors in the space are EMC with their Documentum software, IBM, OpenText, and Oracle.

HRIS Systems

Human resource information systems, or HRIS systems are used to manage a business's employees and data. Some functions that these systems typically include are, software to hire and retain workers, administration functions, scheduling, employee self-service modules, performance record management, and HR planning. Leading vendors include workday ADP, SAP, Oracle, and Kronos.

SCM Systems

The last enterprise system we will talk about is the supply chain management or SCM systems. These systems manage material information and financial data as materials move from suppliers to manufacturers and then finally to customers. Typical functions included with the software are customer requirements modules, purchase order management, and inventory management, warehouse management, and supply management. Some of the leading vendors are SAP, Oracle, JDA Software and IBM. You will note that some vendors compete in many enterprise application areas.

Summary

In summary, enterprise applications are an essential part of the IT industry. Initially, these software packages were so costly that only large corporate implemented these solutions. However, more small and medium-size companies are moving to these solutions. Most vendors now offer cloud-based packages and on-premise solutions. Companies like salesforce.com which only provides a cloud solution are growing at a rapid rate. I hope this section has given you a basic understanding of enterprise applications and why they are an essential part of information technology.

6.0 Database Management Systems

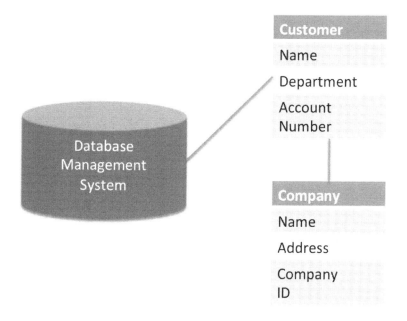

Database management systems are an essential part of today's information technology industry. These systems have been in place since the late 1970s and are a mainstay of most large-scale systems in place in commercial and government systems. Many of today's web-facing ordering and transaction systems have a backend that is a database system that performs the transaction processing.

Database management systems represent a well-known mature technology that can be used to implement a system for almost any size system. Smaller systems may use a desktop database such as Microsoft Access, while larger systems may use a high-end database from vendors such as Microsoft, Oracle, or IBM.

In this chapter, I will start with a discussion of relational databases, which make up the majority of products on the market today. Next, I will then briefly describe the basics of the Structured Query Language or SQL. If you work for a large company or a government agency, you will probably work with an extensive database that your organization runs and maintains. The necessary information in this chapter will give you the basics of how these systems work.

6.1 What is a Relational Database?

In this section, I will describe relational database management systems. I will describe the basic definition of these systems and why they are essential in today's world. I will also explain some advantages of a relational database and some of their limitations. Also, I will briefly describe Structured Query Language or SQL and how to use it with a relational database.

A relational database is a system built for data storage and retrieval based on the relational model. In the relational model, the database organizes data into tables with rows and columns of data. A primary key uniquely identifies each row in a table. Also, a row can contain several columns similar to the design of a typical spreadsheet row. Each column has a unique data type such as an integer, date, string, etc. Tables are then related to each other by establishing relationships using foreign keys.

Example

This figure describes a simple database design with two tables related to each other. This diagram is called an entity relationship diagram and is used by database designers to develop and document these systems.

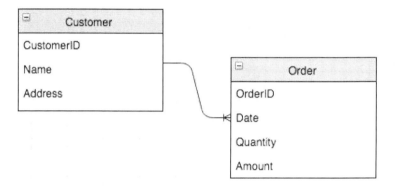

In this example, there is a base table called customer that contains the customer name and address. Also, an order table includes order information for various customers. The diagram indicates there is a one to many relationships between customer and order. One customer can have many orders. ER diagrams allow designers to design and document complex database designs and show the relationships between tables. An extensive database may contain hundreds of tables with many complex relationships. The diagram may cover a large part of a wall in a conference room.

History

The term "relational database" was invented by E.F. Codd while working at IBM in 1970. Codd developed much of the underlying theory of how a relational database would function. He developed the relational model that describes how databases are to entities and relationships and the basic theory of how to query data from these systems using the relational model.

In 1979, Oracle developed the first commercial relational database system. Their business quickly grew, and today Oracle is one of the largest software companies in the world, and the Oracle database system is still one of the market leaders. Other relational databases quickly followed by other vendors including products from IBM, Microsoft, and others.

Advantages

Relational databases have many advantages. One of the primary benefits is they have been around for some time, and they represent a well-known, stable technology. Database management is a routine part of a computer science curriculum and finding skilled programmers that understand database design and implementation is easy to find in most parts of the world. Another significant advantage of most commercial relational database management systems is, they generally include a well-defined robust security model. Almost all software systems require extensive security systems and relational databases offer these as an out of the box configuration item.

Besides these features, relation database systems are designed to efficiently store data and eliminate data redundancies. Eliminating data redundancies is part of the normalization process that Codd developed to design relational databases. This process allows software developers to build complex systems based on these designs. Also, commercial database management systems can scale to handle massive amounts of data. Many of today's data-driven web systems have a relational database as a back-end system to store and process transactions as they come in over the web. Another significant advantage of these systems is they can provide fast retrieval times if the database has an efficient design.

Disadvantages

With the advanced features that most commercial database system offer they can become expensive to buy and deploy. Although there are many open source relational database systems, large corporations still primarily depend on commercial software from leading vendors such as Oracle, Microsoft, and IBM. As these systems scale up the software licensing and support costs can become expensive.

Besides the licensing cost, the design of a large-scale database can be expensive, as well. If a large system consists of hundreds or even thousands of tables, this can be a long and costly process to design and maintain such a system. Skilled database designers and database administrators command high salaries in today's market so a long process of design and maintenance will be an expensive project for most organizations.

Another problem with the design of most software systems today based on relational databases is they can be difficult to modify once they are in production. Often in large systems, it can be expensive and difficult to add even a single column to an existing table.

Even with these limitations relational databases still dominate the landscape of large-scale storage systems for software applications. Other technologies are also on the market such as object-oriented databases and "no SQL" databases, but until these technologies mature relational databases will continue to dominate the market.

SQL

Structured Query Language or SQL is the language used to success relational databases. SQL provides a way to design tables and relationships and a complete Data Definition Language (DDL). Also, SQL also provides a Data Manipulation Language (DML) to allow programmers to insert data, delete data and query the system for results. SQL has evolved over the years to become a complete, robust programming language. There are ISO and ANSI standard versions of SQL that are industry standards.

Normalization

Normalization is the process used to design relational databases. Codd developed this process, and it is a systematic way to decompose the design of the data into corresponding tables and relationships. Each step of this process is used to develop a relational model that accurately describes the system that is being modeled and to remove redundancies in the data and to make it consistent. The steps of normalization are beyond the scope of this book, but I will be covering this in more detail in a book I am writing on database management systems. For this introductory material, the critical point to remember is normalization is the defined process that database designers use to develop and refine relational database designs.

Major Vendors

More vendors are offering database products as the technology changes, but Oracle, Microsoft, and IBM are some of the leading vendors on the market today. Also, these vendors also offer cloud-based versions of their database to provide customers with options to lower their operating costs. This market will continue to evolve as the technology changes and cloud-based systems continue to mature.

Summary

In summary, relation databases remain a large and vital part of the information technology business. Many companies will continue to design and operate a relational database system as a critical part of their IT infrastructure. Relational databases will continue to evolve as the market changes and more companies move to cloud-based technologies.

6.2 Introduction to SQL

In this section, I will provide a brief overview of the Structured Query Language or SQL. SQL is the programming language used for relational database management systems. IBM initially developed SQL in the early 1970s. In the late 1970s, a company which was later to become the Oracle Corporation brought the first commercially available version of SQL to the marketplace. SQL became an ANSI standard in 1986. Even though standards exist for SQL, many vendors still add in their nuances to SQL, so moving code from one database to that of another vendor generally requires some rework.

SQL provides a complete programming language for creating tables in the database, adding data to those tables and the reporting or querying the data in those tables. It also provides commands for updating and deleting data from those tables.

SQL also provides commands for a complete programming language for such things as variables, loops and if statements you would find in a typical programming language like C or Basic. Databases store these complete programs as stored procedures, that are executed at a later time by other programs. Most databases also support the ability to launch applications on various events in the system via a mechanism called a trigger. I will not describe triggers and stored procedures in this section but want to mention them to illustrate the complete programming model provided by SQL.

In the next few sections, I will describe some of the more frequently used by SQL to show you how you would learn the language. The SQL language provides hundreds of commands literally, but in this section, we will get started with just a few key commands.

Create Table

The first command we will discuss is the Create Table statement. This statement is used to create new tables within an existing database. Tables are the primary storage elements of a relational database. Each table has columns of data defined by fields. Each field has a corresponding data type that specifies the data that is stored by the system in those fields. Once this definition is complete, the database stores this data in rows within those tables. This process is very similar to how data stored in a single spreadsheet, with the exception that the data in each column must match the datatype of the specified field. If you look at the following statement, you will notice we are creating a table to store student data, one that has four columns.

```
Create Table Student (
 StudentID int,
 FirstName varchar(40),
 LastName varchar(40),
 BirthDate date
);
```

The above statement creates a table called
student with four columns or fields. The first
one is an ID number for the students which is an
integer value. The next two are the first and last
name which use the string datatype, known as
varchar. The (40) along with the varchar
determines the maximum length of the string.
The last field is the birthdate, and that and uses
a date datatype. Because this the system will
only store valid dates in this field.

Insert Into

Now that we have a table defined we can now load data into that table. This is done with the SQL Insert Into statement. These statements add in 2 new rows to our Student table.

```
/* add in the first student */
INSERT INTO Student (StudentId,
FirstName, LastName, BirthDate)
VALUES (1,'Eric', 'Frick',"1-1-2001");
```

```
/* add in the second student */
INSERT INTO Student (StudentId,
FirstName, LastName, BirthDate)
VALUES (2,'Test', 'Person',"2-2-2002");
```

You will notice the lines starting with the "/*" marks. These are SQL comments and will not be executed by SQL. These are allowed in the code for programmers to make notes and what they are doing to make the code easier to read by other programmers.

If you look at each insert statement, the first part of the statement declares which table this statement is updating. The next part determines the fields or columns that are the target of this insert statement. The last part of the statement contains the data elements for this statement. Note that the order of the data must align with the order of the fields specified.

Select

Now that we have data in our table, we can report or query the data stored in those tables. This SQL Select statement is the command used to produce this report. Listed below is the simplest version of the Select statement: Select * from Student;

This will produce this output:

StudentID	FirstName	LastName	Birthdate
1	Eric	Frick	1-1-2001
2	Test	Person	2-2-2002

The Select statement queries data from the table. The * is a shorthand that says I want the available fields. You can also specify the exact fields you would like to return in the query. The query below is an example of this:
Select FirstName, LastName from Student;

This query will produce this output:

FirstName	LastName
Eric	Frick
Test	Person

Besides filtering the columns, you can also filter the number of rows you would like to return.

Select FirstName,LastName where LastName ='Frick';

This will produce the following output:

FirstName	LastName
Eric	Frick

The 'where' clause allows the select statement to return only rows that meet the filtering condition specified. These can become complex, but here I have illustrated the basic example to get you started.

Update

The SQL update statement allows you to update existing data in a relational database table. The following example would change the last name of Student number 1 from "Frick" to "Fricky." Notice that the update statement also utilizes the where clause.

Update Student Set LastName = 'Fricky' where StudentId=1;

Now, if we issue this SQL Select statement:

Select FirstName, LastName from Student;

This query will produce this output:

FirstName	LastName
Eric	Fricky
Test	Person

The output will reflect our updated data.

Delete

If you would like to remove a row of data from a table, you can use the SQL delete statement. This example will delete the first row in our database.

Delete from Student where StudentId =1;

Now if you issue this select command, you will notice that the first row in the table is no longer there after issuing this query.

Select FirstName, LastName from Student;

This query will produce this output:

FirstName	LastName
Test	Person

Please be careful to add in a 'where' clause to the delete statement. Otherwise, it will delete all the rows in the table.

Drop Table

The last command described in this section is the Drop Table command. This command will delete the table definition and all of its associated data, so be careful with this command. The following command will drop our Student table;

Drop Table Student;

Now if you try to run a select statement against students such as the following:

Select * from Student;

You will get an error saying the table is undefined since we just deleted it.

Summary

In this section, I have given you a basic tutorial on the SQL programming language and its basic syntax. The examples described show you the basic syntax to define tables in

SQL and then populate them with data. You now also know the basic syntax to query, update and delete data from a relational database table. Although SQL can become more complex with a more extensive database additional commands and concepts will build on the basic syntax elements presented here.

7.0 Cloud Computing

Cloud computing is one of the fastest growing areas of information technology today. Many companies and government organizations are moving large-scale systems from their own data centers. What is the motivation behind this? Why would companies want to give up control of some of their vital systems and move to the cloud? I will discuss this and many other issues related to cloud computing in this chapter.

In the first section of this chapter, I will present some basic definitions of cloud computing and some of the basic services offered. I will also describe some of the major advantages and disadvantages of cloud computing. In the next section, I will talk about some of the major vendors in the cloud computing market today.

In the last three sections of this chapter, I will go into more details with Amazon AWS, which is the leading cloud computing vendor in the world today. First, I will give you an overview of the history of Amazon AWS and some services they offer. Next, I will show you how to sign up for a free account with Amazon. After you have your free account, I will show you how to deploy a server on the Amazon AWS cloud.

7.1 What is Cloud Computing?

Cloud computing delivers computing services to remote users over a network. Private clouds are services that are intended to be utilized by a single organization. Either private or public networks can deliver these services. Public clouds provide computing services over the internet and are generally available to anyone with a credit card. Public cloud service providers deliver these services via massively shared data centers. These shared data centers allow cloud service providers the ability to offer services that smaller private companies could not afford to build in their own data centers. Pictured above is one of Microsoft's Azure data centers.

Cloud computing has its roots in some early mainframe services offered to customers in the pre-2000 era. Many early services provided a paid service that users could consume remotely. However, network infrastructure in the during that era limited the number and services that the infrastructure could provide to remote users. Salesforce.com is one of the early pioneers of Software as a Service (SAAS) in 1999. These types of services enabled many companies to implement CRM systems quickly.

Amazon.com launched some of the new Infrastructure as a Service (IAAS) services in 2006, they have since followed up with a large number of cloud services. Microsoft Azure began its cloud services starting in 2010. Since then the leading IT companies now have cloud service offerings. The following diagram predicts that the Cloud Computing market is projected to reach $160 billion by 2020.

Figure 3 from Forbes describes the dramatic growth in cloud-based systems by different areas. I will define these areas later in this chapter.

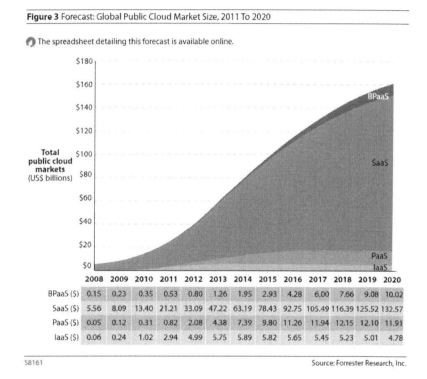

Figure 3 Forecast: Global Public Cloud Market Size, 2011 To 2020

The spreadsheet detailing this forecast is available online.

	2008	2009	2010	2011	2012	2013	2014	2015	2016	2017	2018	2019	2020
BPaaS ($)	0.15	0.23	0.35	0.53	0.80	1.26	1.95	2.93	4.28	6.00	7.66	9.08	10.02
SaaS ($)	5.56	8.09	13.40	21.21	33.09	47.22	63.19	78.43	92.75	105.49	116.39	125.52	132.57
PaaS ($)	0.05	0.12	0.31	0.82	2.08	4.38	7.39	9.80	11.26	11.94	12.15	12.10	11.91
IaaS ($)	0.06	0.24	1.02	2.94	4.99	5.75	5.89	5.82	5.65	5.45	5.23	5.01	4.78

58161

Source: Forrester Research, Inc.

Figure 3 Global Public Cloud Market Size 2011 to 2020

(http://www.forbes.com/sites/louiscolumbus/2015/01/24/roundup-of-cloud-computing-forecasts-and-market-estimates-2015/#41cd412c740c)

7.2 What Are the Advantages of Cloud Computing?

In this section I will describe some of the key advantages of cloud computing and why it is an attractive alternative for hosting major software projects for many companies. I will outline the advantages in four key areas.

Utility Computing

Cloud computing offers a utility model for computing. You only pay for the resources you use, much like your power company. For example, if you have a server running in the cloud, you will probably be charged by the minute. If you do not need the resource 24/7, you can turn it off when you are not using it, and you will not incur charges.

You will, however, pay for the storage costs; however, these costs are generally small as compared to runtime services.

Dynamic Scaling

Also, most cloud systems provide a model where you can quickly scale up your computing needs to meet a dynamic demand. This model is a much more cost-effective way to meet the demands of systems with very dynamic usage patterns.

An example of this is a tax filing system with peak demands around filing times. The system can be set up to automatically add more resources as the load increases and then scale back resources when the load decreases. This feature can be a huge advantage for developers since this technology is easy to access and rarely requires specific coding to take advantage of these services.

Another advantage of cloud computing systems is they generally offer self-provisioning models where end users can provision servers and network resources quickly. Usually, new servers can be built and brought on-line in a matter of minutes. In the physical server world, this can take weeks or even months. This time savings can be a significant advantage to developers who might need to get new code to market quickly.

Disaster Recovery

Another benefit of most cloud systems is that they offer advanced services for failover and disaster recovery. These are generally add-on fees, but they allow companies to consume these services quickly. Many smaller companies cannot afford to build an alternate data center for redundancy.

Standards Compliance

One more advantage of cloud computing is that many providers comply with many industry standard certifications such as HIPAA and PCI. These certifications are very expensive for smaller companies to achieve on their own.

7.3 What are the Limitations of Cloud Computing?

Physical Access

One major limitation of this technology is that you do not have physical access to your data and the servers you have provisioned. Many companies and government organizations require their employees to have access to these physical environments. This requirement is just impossible with the cloud computing model.

If you have systems that have these requirements, you must deploy them on servers that your employees can access. Another limitation is that often you do not control the network resources to connect to the cloud system. If there is a problem with that network, you will not be able to physically access network resources that are in your cloud service provider's data center. Even if your systems are running, they are no good to anyone if you cannot connect to them over a network.

Security Concerns

Another concern for most companies and government agencies is that a third party provides security for these systems that you do not directly control. This situation makes many companies nervous enough not to adopt these systems. By putting provisions in the service providers contract to enact penalties in cases of service failures, you can mitigate some of these risks.

Also, many companies are now adopting a hybrid model where some resources reside in an on-premise data center and the remainder liver in the cloud. In this way, they can pick the environment that best suits your requirements.

7.4 Cloud Computing Service Models

There are three major cloud computing service models, they are:

- Infrastructure as a Service or IAAS
- Platform as a Service or PAAS, and
- Software as a service or SAAS

I will now describe each one of these in more detail.

Infrastructure as a Service

Infrastructure as a Service or IAAS is a way to provide virtualized resources over the internet. This model supports rapid provisioning of servers, routers, network resources, and anything to build your own complete data center in the cloud. Also, many systems provide scripting languages and other resources so much of this work can be automated. This capability allows companies to cut down on the labor required to maintain their server infrastructure. These systems also provide advanced services such as dynamic scaling.

A good example of Infrastructure as a Service is the Google Cloud Platform's Compute Engine Service. The Compute Engine Service allows users to quickly provision servers in the cloud and they are billed by the actual amount of usage. Google bills out their servers on per-second usage. If you turn the server off you will not be billed for runtime services, only the storage cost for the virtual hard disk. The storage cost is very cheap compared to the runtime cost. Other cloud providers such as Microsoft and Amazon offer similar services.

You can read more about the Google Compute engine server here:
https://cloud.google.com/compute/

Platform as a Service

Platform as a Service or PAAS allows customers to build and deploy applications without the complexity of building physical infrastructure and configuring software. For example, Microsoft Azure offers Microsoft SQL server database as a service. With this database service you do not need to build servers or install software, you load your database and tables into this system. However, with most types of services, a rework is often required. Many companies look at these services when building a new system or performing significant upgrades to older systems.

Software as a Service

Software as a Service or SAAS allows an organization to consume entire hosted applications over the intent or private network. With this model, there is no software to install or maintain since the vendor takes complete responsibility for this. There are many examples of this model on the market today. Office 365 from Microsoft fits in this model. Although you can install Office locally on your computer, there are also cloud-based versions of the product that allows you to run Office in a browser. Also, users can store data in the cloud on Microsoft OneDrive, and use email can be stored in the cloud as well. Other examples of SAAS vendors include NetSuite a major ERP vendor, and Service Now which is a cloud-based service and ticketing system for IT shops.

7.5 The Top Ten Cloud Computing Vendors

In this section, I will describe the top 10 Cloud Computing vendors for 2016. This list will continue to change over time, but it will give you an idea of the top companies that are involved. While the demand for cloud computing continues to rise companies are responding to that demand with new and innovative services. Datamation has published their top ten cloud computing vendors for 2016.

Here are the top ten from this list:

- Amazon AWS
- Microsoft Azure
- IBM
- Google Cloud Platform
- SalesForce.com
- Adobe
- Oracle Cloud
- SAP
- Rackspace
- Workday

Not surprisingly, Amazon is on top of the list, but many others on the list are investing heavily and marketing their services aggressively to companies and government agencies. Many companies offer special government only cloud offerings to help secure Federal, State, and local government contracts.

Some companies started with more traditional software and hardware models, but have now branched out into cloud computing.

SalesForce.com makes almost all of its revenue from cloud services and has been enjoying double-digit growth over the last few years.

In the early days of cloud computing, many companies were mostly interested in IAAS or platform offerings from companies like Amazon, Microsoft, Rackspace, and Google, but more SAAS-based offerings from companies such as Salesforce, SAP, and Workday have now seen tremendous growth. Also, many companies are now turning to platforms such as Salesforce as an application development platform, opening up further opportunities for software developers.

The market for cloud computing products and services continues to grow and evolve quickly. The companies on this list are investing heavily in new products and services and are working hard to move up the list. Microsoft alone is spending billions annually in constructing new data centers for Azure. With this competition, the cost of cloud services will continue to drop and will further increase adoption.

7.6 Cloud Computing Quiz

1) Which company is the leading cloud computing vendor in the market today?

    A) Microsoft
    B) Oracle
    C) Amazon
    D) IBM

2) What does SaaS refer to?

    A) Software as a Service
    B) Software analysis system
    C) Software analytics and systems

3) What is IaaS?

    A) Internet Awareness Service
    B) Infrastructure as a Service
    C) Intelligent Advertising Agent Service

4) What is Amazon's cloud system called?

    A) Amazon AWS
    B) The Amazon Cloud System
    C) The Amazon Personal Cloud

5) Salesforce.com is an example of?

    A) IAAS
    B) PAAS
    C) SAAS

6) Having direct physical access to servers is an advantage to cloud computing.

    A) True
    B) False

7.7 Amazon AWS Overview

So, what is Amazon Web services? Amazon Web services cloud computing services delivered by a large number of data centers that Amazon has built on a worldwide basis. Amazon offers the services to both commercial and government customers and is the leading cloud computing vendor in the market today.

Amazon AWS provides regional data centers are on various continents across the globe. These regional data centers or further subdivided into availability zones. By providing these regional data centers and availability zones, Amazon can provide customers with multiple failover options and also locate services closer to their customers.

If we look at a brief history of Amazon, AWS, Amazon Web Services, was launched in 2008. Following the launch of Amazon Web services in 2010, Amazon moved all of its operations to AWS to run its internal business. In 2010, Amazon launched a certification program for both developers and engineers to operate Amazon cloud-based data centers. In 2013, Amazon was awarded the Fedramp certification and did business with the US federal government. Until recently, Amazon did not report AWS income separately from the rest of the company operations, but in 2015 reported Q1 revenues of $1.57 billion.

Since 2008, Amazon has landed some high-profile customers. Two customers that run their web businesses on Amazon's infrastructure are Netflix and Expedia. These companies both run large-scale operations on Amazon services. Amazon also has such customers as Spotify, Comcast, and Coursera. If you look at their website, it will give you more of a complete list of their current customers.

Amazon AWS offers a wide range of cloud computing services. This list of services is growing, and new services are released frequently. Computer services, storage, and content delivery, database services networking and analytics are some of the service offered by Amazon AWS. Besides the services AWS also offers enterprise applications as well as mobile services, Internet of Things, developer tools, and management tools. The last two services listed are security and identity and application services. Each of these service areas has multiple services offered in each area. As you can see from the list, this is a long and comprehensive list of services.

In the next section, I will be demonstrating how to sign up for an account with Amazon and also detailed is free tier usage. Following that, I will show you how to log into the management console in Amazon AWS and create a virtual machine.

In summary, Amazon offers services for infrastructure as a service, platform as a service, and software as a service. We have seen that the service list is very comprehensive. Also, Amazon is the leading cloud service provider in the market today with many high-profile customers.

7.8 Free Account With Amazon AWS

This section describes how to sign up for a free
account for Amazon AWS. Once you sign up,
you can then use their cloud services from the
web console.

Navigate to the AWS web page

First, go to http://aws.amazon.com/free in
your web browser.

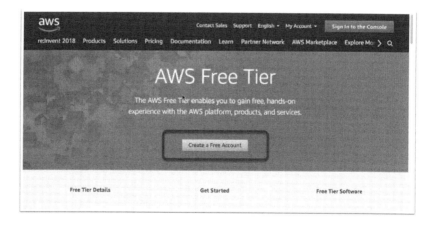

Read about the FREE tier

Next, read about the features of Amazon's free service tier. This trial lasts for 12-months and has limitations on the number of compute hours you can consume and the size of the virtual servers you can provision. These free services change from time to time so scroll through the list to see the complete details.

Click on the Free Tier Button to Get Started

After you have reviewed the list of free services click on the Create a Free Account Button to begin the registration process.

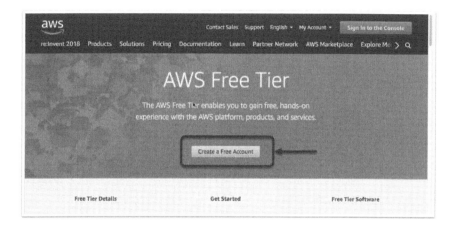

Create your login credentials

Enter your email address as well as your desired password for your account. You will also have to enter in an account name as well. Click the Continue button once you have completed entering this information.

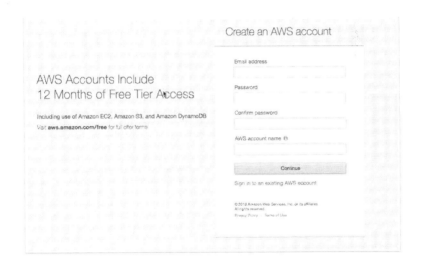

Enter your contact information

Next enter in all of your account information. First, select whether this is a company or personal account. After filling this in, enter the captcha code and then check that you have read the terms and conditions. After completing this, then click the Create Account and Continue button.

Enter your payment information

Now, enter your credit card information and then select the continue button. Even though this is a free account, they still require a credit card number if you use resources outside the free tier. This account will allow you to use resources outside the free ones and Amazon does an excellent job of letting you when you use resources outside the free tier. We will see this in a later chapter when we create a virtual machine with a free account.

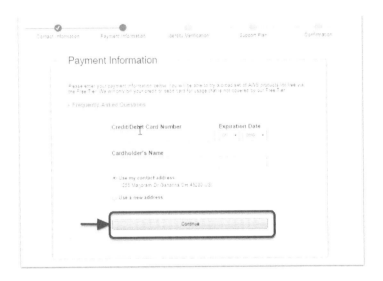

Verify your identity

Next, enter your cell phone number for an identity verification check.

Enter your PIN

Complete the verification

Next, click the Continue to select your Support
Plan button.

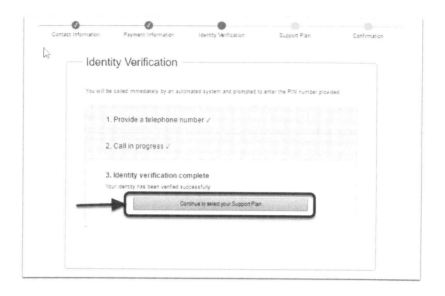

Select your support plan

Select the Basic support plan which Amazon includes for free. The other plans, are paid support plans you can upgrade to later if you need them. For just getting started with the platform, the basic plan is all you must get going.

Complete your selection

After selecting the basic plan, click the
Continue button to move to the next step.

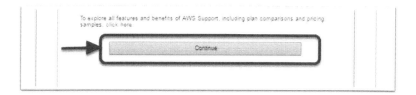

Wait for your verification email

Wait for your verification email, once you have received this you can then sign into your account and use AWS. Click the Sign in to the Console button to use your new account.

Log into your new account

Enter your email address and password and then click the Sign in using our secure server button to log in.

You are now logged in

Now that you are logged in, you can use AWS services Click on the ECS icon to get started. We will cover this in more detail in later lessons. Once you are done using the service, click on the menu under your name to log out.

7.9 How to Create a Virtual Machine in Amazon AWS

Now that you have your account with Amazon AWS, I will describe how you can quickly create a virtual server in the cloud.

Navigate to the AWS Homepage

Go to https://aws.amazon.com. Click the Sign in to the Console button to log in. If you would like to view a video of this process, click here to see this on my YouTube channel.

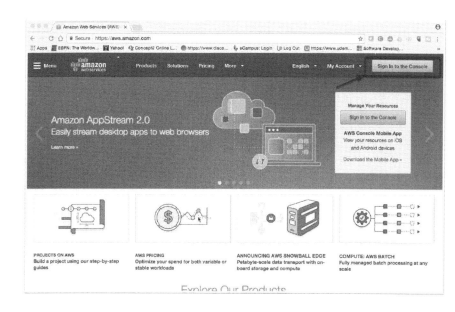

Log in to your Account

Use the username and password you used to sign up for your account.

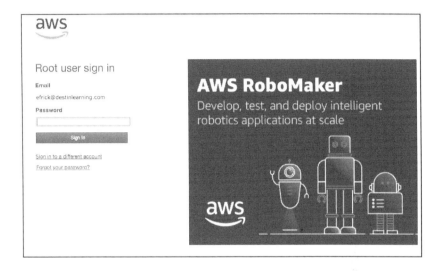

Navigate to the Services Page

Click the services link in the upper left-hand portion of the screen labeled Services.

Click the EC2 link

Once the services are displayed, click the EC2
link to bring up the pages you use to manage
virtual machines.

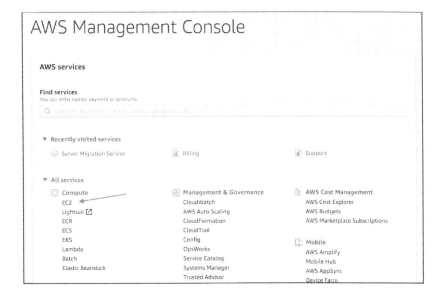

Navigate to the instances page

Click the instances link to open the EC2 instance manager page. On this page you will see the list of machines you already have running (if you have any) and you will have a chance to create a new one there.

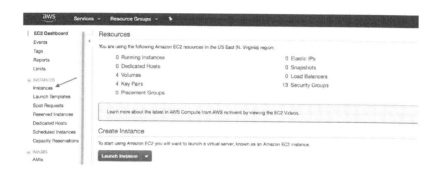

Click the Launch Instance button

Once this page has opened, you can review the status of any other machine in your account. Here I already have several virtual machines created. In your case, you will have a brand-new account, and there will be no machines listed. Once this page has loaded, click the Launch Instance button.

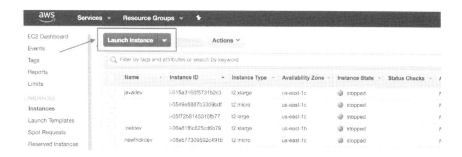

Select the Instance Image

Scroll down through the list and select the instance you would like to create. Here I will use the Windows Server 2016 Base image. Notice the instance types that are free tier eligible have a label indicating that.

Select the Instance Type

This page should default to the t2.micro which is a small, but a free machine to operate. The other types listed are larger machines which you will incur costs for using these. If this computer is not fast enough for your task, you can upgrade it later on the fly. One of the significant advantages of cloud computing is the ease with which you can add resources to your projects. For this exercise select the default. Click the Review and Launch button.

Launch your virtual machine

At this point, you are ready to launch your new virtual machine. The system will warn you about your security group and that it could be made to be more secure. Do not worry about this for this exercise since it is only a development computer. If you want to use this to store more personal data later, I would recommend locking this down at a later time. Click the Launch button to continue.

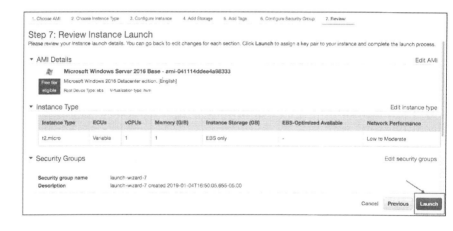

Select the key pair for your machine

You must have a key to launch a new machine and then use that later to retrieve the password. Select to create a new key pair and assign a name for that key. Once you have entered the name, you must download the key to store on your local computer. You will need this later to retrieve the password for your new virtual machine. Click the Download Key Pair button.

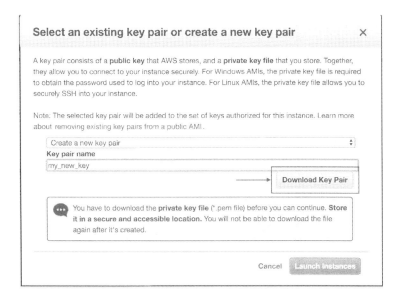

Note where your file is stored

You will need this file later so look in your browser window to note the file location.

Click the Launch Instances button

Now that you have your key file click the
Launch Instances button to begin the build
process.

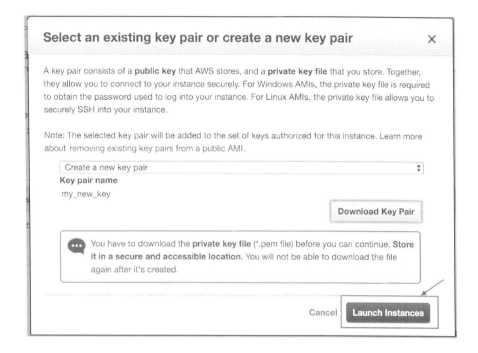

Check the Launch Status

This window will alert you to the status of your new instance. Click the View Instance button at the bottom of the page to return to the instances management page.

Check your new instance status

When you return to this page, you will see the status of your new server. Once the button turns green, your new machine has been created and is running.

Get the windows password

Right mouse click on your new server and then select the Get Windows Password selection from the menu.

Select the Key File

Once this window comes up, select the Choose File button and then select the key file you created in the previous step.

Open the key file

Navigate to where you stored your key file and then click the Open button after you have located the file.

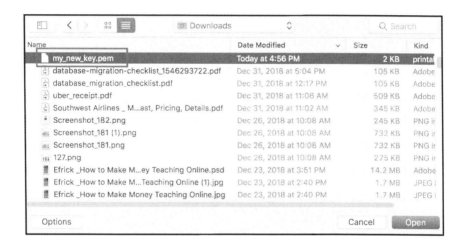

Click the Decrypt Password button

Once the key file has been loaded click the Decrypt Password button to get your Windows system password.

Note your new password

The system has assigned a new password to you which you can view at the bottom of the window. Record this so you can use it to log in to the next step. (You can highlight this to copy it and paste it into a file on your system to make it easier to manage or you can write it down.) Click the close button when finished recording your password.

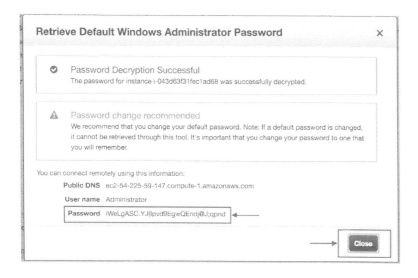

Click the Connect button

Now that you have your password, you can now connect to your running computer. Right mouse click on the running computer line and then click the Connect link from the menu.

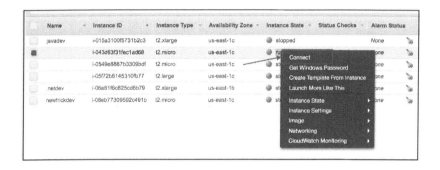

Download the Remote Desktop File

Click the Download the Remote Desktop file button so you can use remote desktop to log in to your new computer.

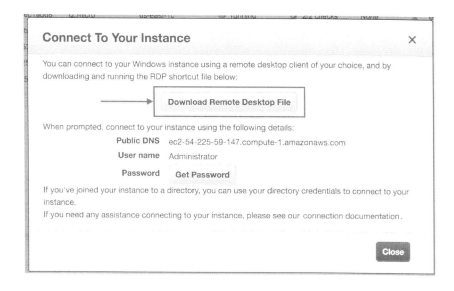

Navigate to the remote desktop file

Once the file download completes, open the directory where the file and double click on the file to open the remote desktop software. Note you must have remote desktop software installed on your computer. Windows PCs should have this software already installed. It is a free download from Microsoft and is also available for the Mac in the App Store. You can get this from the following link for Mac:

https://itunes.apple.com/us/app/microsoft-remote-desktop-10/id1295203466?mt=12

Here is the link for the Windows version of the software in case you need it:

https://www.microsoft.com/en-us/p/microso ft-remote-desktop-preview/9nblggh3oh88?ac tivetab=pivot:overviewtab

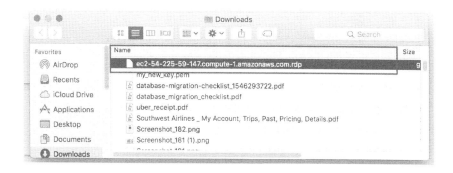

Log into your new machine

Use the password you recorded in the previous step. (It is long and difficult to type in for the first time.) After you log in, you can use standard Windows commands to reset the password to something that is easier for you to manage. I recommend pasting the password into a document and then printing it out to log in for the first time. The password is complicated to write down correctly.

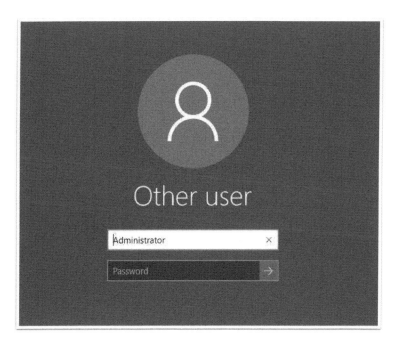

You should now be logged in

If all goes well, your computer is running, you should now be logged in, and you can use your computer for anything you want. Even though this is a free tier computer, you only have a limited number of free hours so shut it down when you are not using it. You can either shut it down from the server or from the Amazon command line.

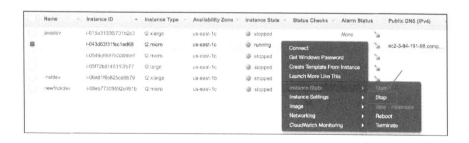

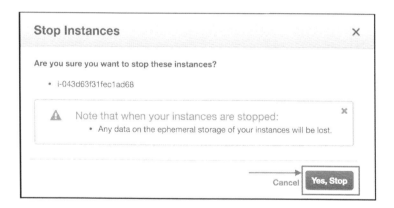

8.0 Computer Security

Computer security has become a major area within the information technology business over the last several years. Before computers become connected to the internet, most companies only needed to worry about securing their computers in their own data centers and did not need to worry so much about people hacking into their computers from the outside world. Instead, most corporate data centers were concerned about providing physical security for their computers and protecting against physical break-ins and protecting their data centers against physical damage such as severe weather or fires.

Today, protecting corporate computers is a more complex task since most major companies in the world do business over the internet. Groups of people are now actively trying to break into corporate and government computers to steal valuable information or to perform a malicious task to bring computer operations to a halt. There have been many high-profile security breaches against large corporations in the last few years that have resulted in these companies losing millions of dollars. These breaches not only cost companies lost revenue, but they may also lose much of their customer base.

Home computer users also face similar threats. Although home computers rarely have a vast treasure trove of sensitive customer data that corporate computers have, they might have just enough data to allow a criminal to run up a big bill against your credit card accounts or piece together enough data to steal your identity. Either of these scenarios represents a bad outcome for a typical home computer user. Also, since more users now have mobile devices, protecting users has now become even more complicated.

In this chapter, I will describe some of the significant threats facing home computer users today and some steps that can take for necessary protection. Unfortunately, even though protections have improved for computers, the threats are also becoming more frequent and more sophisticated.

8.1 Computer Security Threats

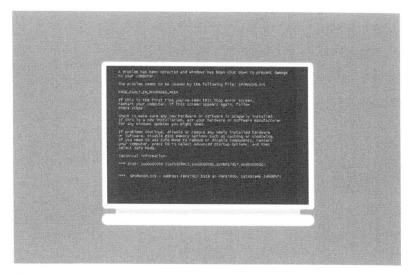

Most home computers' settings allow your computer to accept these updates over the internet regularly. However, these automatic updates can also be disabled from the administration screen. Many users turn these off since the constant stream of updates can become annoying. Turning these updates off will allow your computer to become more vulnerable.

Spyware

Spyware is a software installed on your computer that attempts to gain knowledge about you without alerting you that the software is active. Spyware comes in many forms. Some of it may track your internet usage patterns, but other forms may try to log the keystrokes you are typing in (keylogger) and attempt to steal information you are typing in such as an account number or password. There are many special purpose spyware removal and monitoring programs on the market today. Installing one of these and keeping it updated will help prevent you from being attacked by this software.

Spam

Spam is the large collection of junk mail that most home computer users get in their email. Much of this email is harmless, but email is a significant way for hackers to distribute computer viruses and malware. Although major email vendors such as Microsoft and Google continuously monitor their email for these issues, bad things still slip through the filters. Having a good Spam filter on your home computer will help prevent these attacks. Another good tactic is to keep all of your emails in the Cloud on a system such as Gmail and never download it to your local computer. One of the best tips is never to download or open an email message if you do not know what it is or who sent it. Just delete these messages and do not take the risk of opening them.

Malware

Malware represents a broad class of malicious software that can harm your computer. Malware distributes itself to other users through a number of means such as email, thumb drives and other infected media, or software installed over the internet. Some malware can be very destructive and might attempt to delete data from your computer, while other types will try to steal data from various parts of the computer. Having a good commercial grade anti-virus software is usually the best line of defense against these threats.

Phishing

Phishing attacks are a user posing as someone else in an attempt for you to give up vital personal information. In this scam, a user will send you an email that looks like your bank or someone you do business with on a regular basis. The email will seem like the real thing and may be very convincing. Inside that email will be a link that does not go to the actual bank but to some fraudulent site. They will ask you to click on that link and log in. The login will fail since it is not the real system, but the criminals have now captured your username and password. Once they have done this, they will use the account to their financial advantage. One way to combat this is to examine the link you are being sent to before you click on it. If you do not recognize the link (like mybank.com) do not continue with the process. Go to your bank independently and call them to verify the letter is legitimate. Companies already doing business with you do not ask you for personal information over the internet.

Summary

In this section, I have briefly described some of the more common threats that face home computer users today. It illustrates the significant growth in threats that computer systems are facing. Although the software programs that protect computers are better than they were a few years ago, the threats continue to improve and multiply.

9.0 The Future of Computing

In this chapter, I will talk about the future of computing. This topic can be broad, so I just selected a few of the more popular trends in the market today to discuss.

Many trends in the IT industry have gotten started, but the growth in these trends, products, and services will continue to accelerate. Some of the major trends are:

- Continued growth in cloud computing
- The growth in IoT, Internet of Things
- Robotic systems
- Digital Assistants
- Artificial intelligence
- Computer security

Let's go through each of these in more detail.

Cloud Computing

The first area is the continued growth of cloud computing. Major service providers like Amazon and Microsoft will continue to push the market for cloud services. Amazon and Microsoft are the number one and number two cloud providers on the market today, and they will continue to push the envelope with new products and services, and prices will continue to drop. Major companies and government organizations will continue their move to the cloud to save money on their operations. With all this growth in cloud computing, new competitors will enter the market and prices will continue to draw for the services.

IoT

The next area I will talk about this Internet of Things or IoT. The money invested in the Internet of Things is expected to grow steadily over the next ten years. Cloud providers such as Amazon and Microsoft are already offering low-cost services to help software developers and integrate systems into devices. The number of connected devices will number in the billions over the next ten years as more and more of these systems come online. The systems will present tremendous opportunities for software companies in software developers. Voice control of these systems is becoming commonplace, and there is already a lot of work underway in integrating devices such as Amazon's Alexa to drive home control systems.

Robotic Systems

Besides software controlled through voice commands, a large amount of work is already underway on a wide variety of robotic systems. Some high-profile work has been going on with Google and the number of automobile companies developing the self-driving car. Control systems have been around for some time and have been used on aircraft systems for many years already. Investment in developing these systems will continue to grow over the next several years. You will see more applications for household robotic systems. Some small examples of these are smart systems like the Roomba vacuum that can learn to navigate your home. As the price of control systems continues to drop, you will see more for home use. Also, industrial robots will continue to become smarter and more flexible in being integrated into production systems.

Digital Assistants

Many have been predictions for many years that digital assistants will someday become popular. The technology has never taken off in the past but is now becoming much more popular with devices such as Amazon's Alexa. You will see these devices in use with automation control systems as this technology continues to mature. More competitors are entering the smart market such as Microsoft, Google, and a host of other companies. You will also see this technology integrated into other form factors such as wearable devices and devices integrated with appliances and other household items. You will see several products introduced over the next couple of years in this market.

Artificial Intelligence

Another area that has been researched over many years, but has not produced a large number of commercial products is artificial intelligence. Just now you are seeing commercial software companies beginning to include AI products in their commercial offerings. Salesforce has just released a product called Einstein that allows artificial intelligence modules to help companies process their sales and CRM data to make intelligent choices about their marketplace. Other companies such as Microsoft and Google are working on similar products. These applications will become more commonplace over the next few years.

Computer Security

The last area I will talk about is computer security. With the growth in cloud-based systems and the growth of the internet, there is a tremendous need for IT security personnel and products. There is a shortage of IT security professionals, and the shortage is causing a rise in personnel salaries. This shortage is also prompting companies to look for security products and appliances that can help them defend their systems from unwanted attacks. The worldwide for demand for IT security services continues to rise.

Summary

In summary, the IT business continues to change rapidly. New products and services are continually introduced to the market by computer vendors, and IT services companies, which can sometimes cause unpredictable changes in the demand for other products. These trends present tremendous opportunities for programmers, software development companies, and personnel. I hope this material has given you some ideas about some of the significant trends in the IT business and will give you some ideas on things that might help your future career.

10.0 Summary

Thank you so much for reading this book. I hope it has given you a good start on your journey to learning more about computer science and software development. As I mentioned in the introduction, this is the first book in a series of books designed to train entry-level software developers. If you have suggestions for improvements for this class, please contact me as I would love to hear from you. Also, please leave a review for me so I can continually make this book better. Thank you again, and I hope to see you again soon.

11.0 About the Author

Eric Frick

I have worked in software development and IT operations for 30 years in positions including Software Developer, Software Development Manager, Software Architect and as an Operations Manager. For the last five years have I taught evening classes on various IT related subjects at several local universities. I currently work as a Cloud Training architect for Linux Academy (https://linuxacademy.com) developing cloud-based certification courses. In 2015 I founded destinlearning.com, and I am developing a series of online courses and books that can provide practical information to students on various IT and software development topics.

12.0 More From Destin Learning

Thank you so much for your interest in this book. I hope it has given you a good start in the exciting field of Information Technology. You can see more from my YouTube channel where I am continuing to post free videos about software development. If you subscribe to my channel you will get updates as I post new material weekly:

http://youtube.com/destinlearning

You can also sign up for my newsletter at http://destinlearning.com where I will send out updates on new material. Thank you again and good luck with your future with Information Technology!

Appendix Quiz Answers

Binary Numbers Quiz

1) 10011001
2) 51
3) 1554057925
4) 1011001001010001
5) True

Quiz 2 Computer Hardware Quiz

D -> Power Supply
A-> CPU
F-> Motherboard
C-> RAM
B-> Hard Disk
E-> System Bus

5.2 SDLC Quiz

1) A
2) C
3) B
4) A
5) B
6) B

5.3 eCommerce Quiz

1) B
2) A
3) C
4) A
5) A

7.6 Cloud Computing Quiz

1) C
2) A
3) B
4) A
5) C

Made in the USA
Middletown, DE
05 December 2023

44636314R00123